OCCUPY

An Anthology of Encouragement, Discovery and Inspiration

Compiled by
Andrea M. Renfroe

The Prophetic Pen
www.thepropheticpen.org

Copyright © 2020 by Andrea M. Renfroe

With exception to scripture references, quotes from individuals or published works, all rights are reserved, and no part of this publication may be reproduced, scanned, distributed, stored in a retrieval system, or transmitted in any form or by any means without express written permission from the publisher.

Holy Bible, New Living Translation, copyright © 1996, 2004, 2015 by Tyndale House Foundation. Used by permission of Tyndale House Publishers, Inc., Carol Stream, Illinois 60188. All rights reserved.

The Holy Bible, New International Version®, NIV® Copyright © 1973, 1978, 1984, 2011 by Biblica, Inc.™ Used by permission. All rights reserved worldwide.

Scripture quotations taken from the Amplified® Bible (AMP), Copyright © 2015 by The Lockman Foundation Used by permission. www.Lockman.org.

Scripture taken from the New King James Version®. Copyright © 1982 by Thomas Nelson. Used by permission. All rights reserved.

Scripture quotations marked TPT are from The Passion Translation®. Copyright © 2017, 2018 by Passion & Fire Ministries, Inc. Used by permission. All rights reserved. ThePassionTranslation.com.

Scripture quotations marked MSG are taken from *THE MESSAGE*, copyright © 1993, 2002, 2018 by Eugene H. Peterson. Used by permission of NavPress. All rights reserved. Represented by Tyndale House Publishers, Inc.

Scripture taken from The Voice™. Copyright © 2008 by Ecclesia Bible Society. Used by permission. All rights reserved.

Editing by The Write Legacy LLC, www.thewritelegacy.com
Scribes Mobilize™ Logo Design by Benford Stallmacher, Authentic DNA Studio, www.authenticdnastudio.wixsite.com

Responsibility for the information and views expressed in this publication rests entirely with the author(s) and do not necessarily reflect the views of the publisher. The publisher disclaims all liability for the information and views presented.

Library of Congress Control Number: 202092007

Printed in the United States of America

ISBN-10: 0-9834520-4-0
ISBN-13: 978-0-9834520-4-1

DEDICATION

To Scribes Mobilize members, I appreciate each one of you. Your presence has enhanced my life and helped bring me to this abundant place in ministry. As you continue to gain ground along your scribal journey, remember to embrace transformation and advocate for it in yourself first and subsequently in every place the Lord grants you access.

Occupy

Acknowledgements

◆

To my husband, Telly Renfroe. Thank you for enduring with me. I know I can work a nerve sometimes with my affinity to detail and need for things to be just right. I am grateful for you. Your ability to look beyond my nuances and indulge me while bringing balance when I start *"doing too much"* is a rarity. You know me well and I thank you for handling that insight with care and wisdom. I love you honey!

To my mentor, Apostle Theresa Harvard Johnson. Thank you for setting a righteous example of Apostolic Mentorship. There is so much I can say about what your presence in my life has produced. I'm sure I'll write a book about it one day. But for now, I'll say this, you've helped me navigate many uncharted waters. This anthology is just one example. With your assistance and encouragement, I was able to cross the finish line not just for the sake of publishing another book but to set a standard for building a scribal community and righteous publishing. I am truly grateful for you!

To my sister, Marquita Everson. You know *"how we do"*; overemphasis on details, the need for everything to convey the intended message, and doing whatever's necessary to make it happen even if that means not eating or sleeping.

Thank you for making me laugh about these quirks and for your feedback through this process.

To Apostle Bernard Boulton, fellow scribe and big brother in Christ. Thank you for being a part of this project and for your invaluable input at various stages. I appreciate your willingness to help with no expectations. You move with sincerity and you embody God's heart for family. It is an honor to call you brother.

To Bernadine Okoro, an original Scribes Mobilize member. Thank you for your feedback concerning various aspects of this project. Your assistance definitely helped make this precious endeavor a success. You are a gem. Thank you!

To the contributing authors. On the strength of God's instructions to me, you took a chance to participate in this project. You entrusted me with a part of you in written form. I did not and do not take that entrustment lightly. I pray this project honors you and that the Scribal Anointing descend upon you, arise within you and break forth through you according to Matthew 13:52.

Table of Contents

Acknowledgements v

Preface 9

Breathe Again 23
Kimberly Cabbagestalk

Freedom isn't Free 29
Elizabeth Kampororo

Break these Cords 33
Bernadine Okoro

Forward, March! 47
Marquita Everson

Barren and Pregnant with God's Love 53
Renee Joseph

The Body 59
Sade McAllister

Redemptive Reflections: Career 65
Dianna Davis-Small

Possess the Land 85
Tanya Stephenson

Breakthrough and Overcome 91
LaShaun O'Bryant

Occupying the Spheres of Ministry and Marketplace 97
Bernard Boulton

About the Compiler 105

Enduring Excellence 107

Preface

◆

"In the beginning...God said let there be light..." Genesis 1:1, 3 NLT

On June 24, 2017, Apostle Theresa Harvard Johnson, the progenitor of *The Scribal Anointing*®, came to the Washington, DC, Maryland, and Virginia (DMV) region on assignment. The transformational deposit God used her to release reminded me of this region's significance, illuminated why scribes in this area must be activated; and provoked me to take my place as a commander of the city.

Washington, DC is the heart of America, the nucleus for national governance, and the helm of worldwide influence. As I thought on these realities, I began to understand better that a KEY to transforming our nation is to awaken sleeping scribes (sleeping giants) and help them personally embrace transformation. From this stable place, they are equipped to intentionally reproduce transformation in their families, communities, regions and ultimately impact the nation and the world.

Although I didn't have details or a well laid out plan, I knew I had to do something. After a time of reflection and picturing what transformation looks like, Deuteronomy 1:6-8 came to me:

> *"When we were at Mount Sinai, the Lord our God said to us, 'You have stayed at this mountain long enough. It is time to **BREAK CAMP** and move on. **GO TO** the hill country of the Amorites and to all the neighboring regions—the Jordan Valley, the hill country, the western foothills, the Negev, and the coastal plain. Go to the land of the Canaanites and to Lebanon, and all the way to the great Euphrates River. Look, I am giving all this land to you! **GO IN** and **OCCUPY** it, for it is the land the Lord swore to give to your ancestors Abraham, Isaac, and Jacob, and to all their descendants.'" Deuteronomy 1:6-8 NLT (emphasis added)*

On July 15, 2017, as a response to God's call and without pomp and circumstance, I launched DMV Scribes Mobilize with a Facebook group page and a small strategy session.

"...go...to the land that I will show you..." Genesis 12:1 NIV

A little over two years after launching, I began to sense the need for a shift. Monthly strategy sessions were consistent. The content was adequate and provoking, some members were growing in their knowledge and understanding of *The Scribal Anointing®* and the manifestation of it in and upon their lives. Yet, it was clear we'd come to a fork in the road as a collective. Pockets of individual growth did not translate to overall growth and production and thus, a change was warranted.

I understood that organizations and groups experience ebbs and flow over time. People join, people leave, needs change, learning levels and appetites fluctuate, focus shifts, etc... But I admittedly struggled a bit with this realization because when you have an assignment, seeing it wean or not blossom into what you imagined it would be can be extremely disappointing. I didn't know exactly what to do, but I did know I could not continue pushing forward with old methodologies or fighting to hold on to something meant to segue into or support something greater; the vision.

We do ourselves and others a great disservice when we entertain and elevate supporting activities and assignments above the appointed vision. Initially I thought DMV Scribes Mobilize was the vision. But God made it clear that Life Keys Training Center (LKTC), the budding organization I founded in 2016, was (and is) the vision and that DMV Scribes Mobilize is an appendage to it. He further clarified that DMV Scribes Mobilize was not to be done away with but to be done differently. In other words, I had to put it in its proper place.

"Who are those who fear the Lord? He will show them the path they should choose." Psalm 25:12 NLT

Customarily, the last few months of each year are set aside for introspection, reflection, inventory, and rest. All such activities are preparation for the coming year. Following reconstructive foot surgery at the end of October 2019 (another reason for the set-aside time), I began to prepare for 2020.

Occupy

The first and most distinct directive I received for 2020 was what you hold in your hands; a group project. The purpose behind it was multifaceted:

1. Demonstrate koinonia. Many use the words ecclesia and koinonia interchangeably. However, they are entirely different and distinct. Ecclesia describes a group, be it believers gathering for worship or the body of Christ. Within the group, unity may be desired but it isn't required. In contrast, koinonia describes the intimate relationship and oneness amid the ecclesia. In other words, the group members desire genuine fellowship and based on sincere intent, they operate in ways that benefit and advance the group. It is unfortunate that God's heart for family and oneness is often ransacked by individualism. There is absolutely nothing wrong with allowing the unique expression of God to shine through. However, people contort and use it as leverage to be seen, heard, elevated, and worshipped instead of using it for God's glory and the edification of His people. God knows we can accomplish more when our hearts are knit together, when we are united in fellowship and when we are one in the Spirit. This project is a testament to what can happen when believers intentionally decide to move succinctly as one mechanism, one unit, one body.

2. Establish a record in the earth and a memorial that heralds *"finished work"* for the contributing authors. I've learned that having a finished work in hand helps to:

    - Dismantle intimidation, fear and limitations (self-imposed and otherwise) and gives the individual hope concerning their assignments be they scribal or non-scribal

    - Provide a blueprint for personal efforts should they chose to publish in the future

3. Introduce the public to the contributing authors and their God-given uniqueness. Some have congregations or ministries, some have businesses, some have a combination of those things, and some are still discovering what God has entrusted to them. Nevertheless, all of them are important and I believe it is proper to encourage, honor and celebrate them no matter where they are in their journey.

The second directive I received was to require a greater level of engagement from scribes through a "Call to Action". Following each monthly strategy session, a call to action (self-analysis) is given that requires scribes to meditate on the lesson and to activate their pens by writing out:

1. Where they were before the lesson in terms of understanding and application

2. Where they are now that they have new information and how they will proceed with it

This approach placed the burden of growth on the scribe and forced them to take their transformation process more seriously. Specifically, our time together was more than a moment in time to learn; it was an opportunity to wrestle with the content for the cause of ensuring growth and not a temporary change. Although the essence of this mandate was always in place, this particular change carried with it greater weight and more accountability.

"...So he went up and looked and said, "There is nothing." Elijah said, "Go back..." I Kings 18:43 NLT

In the midst of major family responsibilities and a job change, COVID-19 descended on the world and everything shifted. I, too, shifted and began holding online strategy sessions. After a few months, DMV Scribes Mobilize still seemed disjointed from my vantage point. While God made it clear at the end of 2019 that DMV Scribes Mobilize was to be done differently, and while I moved in that direction, I didn't fully comprehend what the way forward looked like.

In an effort to really focus on what I should do, I discontinued DMV Scribes Mobilize activities (with exception to this project) and pulled back to do a thorough assessment. The goal was to completely search myself and analyze the group; identify what works, what doesn't work and what needs to be incorporated to help move members (current and future) out of stagnation and into a masterful command of their scribal metron.

During my assessment, God revealed that the approach I'd taken was good. However, it was missing one KEY component. The component was ministry to the whole person which aligns with LKTC's vision and echoes its mission:

- Vision: *We are a relational organization that advocates for and assists with personal and corporate transformation.*

- Mission: *We aim to unlock and develop (build) whole people (spirit, soul, body) who impact and transform their respective areas of influence.*

This is where all of the pieces snapped into place for me.

"Then he opened their minds to understand..." Luke 24:45 NLT

I'd been focusing on trying to help scribes move out of stagnation and into a masterful command of their scribal metron when I should have been trying to help them and countless others move out of stagnation and into a masterful command of their lives. The latter helps achieve the former. I knew this and was actually walking this out with a few scribes. But for some reason, I hadn't grasped the fact that this should be the rule and not the exception.

First, I had to realize that "DMV" was a limit as it was a description of the inaugural region for the group but not an indication of the ordained reach. Second, I did not understand that I didn't have to force it into a box as some kind of stand-alone entity separate from LKTC. Providing scribe specific content is not a detraction from LKTC's vision and mission; it is, in fact, an expression or extension of it. WOW! What a relief to have that established in my mind and my heart.

From this place of clarity, I was able to properly identify Scribes Mobilize as a LKTC program where I specifically facilitate transformation by:

- Awakening and connecting scribes to their biblical history and legacy,

- Grounding and stabilizing scribes in their prophetic identity; and;

- Activating and launching scribes into their present-day responsibilities.

These objectives are accomplished through:

1. Instruction. Scribes receive biblical and practical instruction during periodic strategy sessions to help them navigate their scribal journey.

2. Outings. Scribes visit various historical sites, government offices and other relevant locations to identify scribal functions and activities in society and to observe the relation to their scribal history and legacy, to determine what their specific scribal assignments may look like once completed, and to gain insight into the type of impact their scribal contributions may have on their sphere of influence.

3. Community Events and Activities. Scribes share their gifts by participating in community events hosted by LKTC and other entities throughout their community. This allows for authentic involvement and engagement with those they are called to assist and impact with transformation.

4. Annual publication. Scribes and special guests collaborate to produce a project that demonstrates koinonia, celebrates the contributors and highlights Scribes Mobilize. *OCCUPY* is our debut publication.

"...but I press on to take hold of that for which Christ Jesus took hold of me." Philippians 3:12 NIV

Christ is our firm foundation (1 Corinthians 3:11). From Him, in Him and through Him, we are mandated to herald and demonstrate who He is in the earth. Transformation is my portion, my message. While the message of transformation is captured throughout the bible, the distinct pattern laid out in Deuteronomy 1:6-8 is the thrust behind everything I teach and how I've been sanctioned to build.

> *"When we were at Mount Sinai, the Lord our God said to us, 'You have stayed at this mountain long enough. It is time to **BREAK CAMP** and move on. **GO TO** the hill country of the Amorites and to all the neighboring regions—the Jordan Valley, the hill country, the western foothills, the Negev, and the coastal plain. Go to the land of the Canaanites and to Lebanon, and all the way to the great Euphrates River. Look, I am giving all this land to you! **GO IN** and **OCCUPY** it, for it is the land the Lord swore to give to your ancestors Abraham, Isaac, and Jacob, and to all their descendants.'" Deuteronomy 1:6-8 NLT (emphasis added)*

Let's take a quick look at this pattern. After an 11-day journey morphed into 40 years of wandering, God instructed Moses to remind the Children of Israel concerning the way forward. God's instructions illuminated four very specific and powerful components that cohesively depict the transformation process:

- Break Camp
- Go to
- Go in
- Occupy

In my forthcoming book *Destination Transformation: A Pattern of Sonship*, I delve into each of the four components. Because "occupy" is the theme and title of this project, I want to highlight a specific point here.

Occupy is a dynamic word with multiple meanings and layers. I believe one of its most widely known meanings is; *"to take possession of."*[1] Using this meaning in terms of relationship with God, we can safely conclude that occupy is about moving from immaturity to maturity, from apprenticeship to mastery, from servanthood to **SONSHIP** (Galatians 4:7, Ephesians 4:15).

God intends for us to grow up into the full stature and measure of Christ (Ephesians 4:13). Accordingly, occupy is an emphatic declaration that no matter where a person finds him or herself in the transformation process, to occupy is the objective.

---

[1] Strong, J. (1996). Yarash. In *The new Strong's complete dictionary of Bible words* (pp. 396-397). Nashville, TN: Thomas Nelson

"For whatever was written in earlier times was written for our instruction, so that through endurance and the encouragement of the Scriptures we might have hope and overflow with confidence in His promises." Romans 15:4 AMP

You may be wondering why I shared so many details about my process with Scribes Mobilize. Well, in the absence of history, I believe the present is bleak and the future incomprehensible.

Also, many times, we pick up and read books without knowing the story behind the story. Backstory is important because it provides context to what is currently happening and thereby enhances our reading experience. It may also contain KEYS that release something we need (or will need) specific to our scribal journey or life in general.

Lastly, I wanted to provide an example of what it looks like to navigate the transformation process and to drive home the point that we must walk what we talk and teach what we preach. I don't just advocate for transformation in others, it is the message I've been entrusted with and the message I am first partaker of. I intend to be mature. I intend to be a master and I intend to be a full-grown son of God because He created, ordained and called me to OCCUPY! He has called you to do the same.

An Anthology of Encouragement, Discovery and Inspiration

"...encourage one another and build each other up..."
I Thessalonians 5:11

The gems within these pages reveal people at different points in life and distinct places in the transformation process. Despite their differences, they share a common objective and that is to answer God's call to **OCCUPY**. Their work ranges from encouragement to poetry, prayers to declarations, and testimonies to heartfelt insight. No matter your literary inclination, I am confident you will find something that provokes you to answer the call as well.

"Love each other with genuine affection, and take delight in honoring each other." Romans 12:10

It is my pleasure and distinct honor to present to some and introduce to others, Scribes Mobilize members and special guests.

With great expectation,

Andrea M. Renfroe
Life Keys Training Center, Founder

Breathe Again
Kimberly Cabbagestalk
Original Scribes Mobilize Member

◆

*"The Spirit of God has made me;
the breath of the Almighty gives me life."*
Job 33:4 NIV

Over the past few months, it has become clear that the Lord is calling His people back to Himself. Times of intimate fellowship with the Father has long been suffocated by the busyness of life. Even our commitments to the routine rituals of church life have kept many in a high-performance mode for so long that time to forge genuine relationship has become non–existent. With the recent pandemic plaguing the nations, business, as usual, has been put on pause, leaving people more time for reflection on what matters most. The church has finally left the building and has scrambled to find ways to reach people in unconventional ways. Ministry is being targeted at the masses through social media and other digital platforms. People that haven't been to church in a long time have been able to partake in worship experiences in the privacy of their own homes. Ministries that, at one time, avoided social media for fear of losing their weekly crowds have been pushed into social media ministry for the very same reason. The church has been mobilized.

Could this be the end of an era and the beginning of another? It remains to be seen.

At the beginning of this new decade, there were so many declarations about the clear vision and revelation that would be upon us because -- after all, twenty-twenty vision is optimum sight. I wonder how many of us like what we see now?

I could never have imagined the things that have been uncovered and revealed. One of the significant revelations during this season has been the overwhelming racial disparities, injustice, prejudices, and systematic racism which not only operate in the nation but ashamedly in the church. It has been hard to watch world leaders and church leaders that I have admired for years choose politics over people. It has been both disappointing and eye-opening. Yet, there is a glimmer of hope. You see, I believe that what God reveals, He also heals.

There has been a common phrase resounding all over the earth as the people cry out for justice and equality — "I can't breathe." The ability to breathe is synonymous with living. From the first man, Adam (Gen. 2:7) until now, God has sustained every human being on the earth with his Ruach (breath, wind). To be denied, this fundamental human right is an assault against God and humanity. As I watched people protest in the streets, I began to reflect on the many breathless moments I've encountered as a woman of destiny and purpose pursuing the things that God has for me. I thought about the times when the demonic systems disguised as spiritual coverings aligned against me to keep a knee on my neck in an effort to prevent me from breathing life into my God-given assignments. I experienced destiny suppression in so many ways that I found myself lifeless and gasping for the wind of God to rescue me. Feeling the suffocation of rejection, denial, and betrayal, I was thrust into the presence of God for healing and restoration. The more time I spent in His presence, my lungs began to fill with air again. I began to breathe again. The breath of God began to inhabit a new vision as my kingdom assignments began to unfold.

In the aftermath of the COVID-19 pandemic, I believe there will be a remnant of people that will emerge from the presence of God to usher in a new era of the kingdom of heaven on earth. We will begin to see the people of God vacating places of desolation where they have been held captive by religion and the expectations of men in exchange for areas of fruitfulness, abundance, and overflow. They will vacate their identities as slaves to a tradition which has obstructed their view of God and interrupted their moments of sweet communion for far too long. The chaos of this world has thrust them back into the secret place of the Most High (Psalm 91:1 KJV) and He has revealed His secrets to them. The secrets that bring soul healing and soul prosperity are their portion and they will not settle for anything less. They will finally breathe again. Those breathless moments under the oppressive systems that made them feel ashamed for choosing to obey God in spite of man's disapproval will be a thing of the distant past. They will arise and demonstrate the kingdom as they fulfill their kingdom assignments. They will restore purity back to the preaching of the gospel that will put the merchandisers to shame. I just have one question. Will you be counted as one sent from His presence?

In His presence, the restructuring and course-correcting of destinies are taking place. Racism, prejudices, and systems that glorify elitism and separatism are being dethroned in His presence. He is reigniting the passion for seeing His body unified (fitly joined together) and built in love (Ephesians 4:16) in His presence. Every thought and imagination that has systematically sabotaged His divine purpose, visions, and dreams for them are being purged in His presence. God is placing His seal of approval upon them, and they will emerge with boldness. Being affirmed in the presence of God will cancel the cravings for validation from man.

This has been a very peculiar time in the history of modern civilization. I cannot remember a time when people all over the world have been so impacted simultaneously. At the same time, I have never seen a time when so many people were postured for change. Our political leaders have failed us. Our justice system has failed us. Our financial systems and healthcare systems are struggling to sustain us. It sounds like the trials of Job. He lost everything and was stricken in his health. His whole world had collapsed around him, and yet he decided not to curse God and die. He knew the God who gave him breath would send a fresh wind to restore all that was lost.

I declare that the wind of God is coming to your life to resuscitate your dreams and give you hope for the future. No matter what has been lost or lacking, you will experience a whirlwind recovery. The life-giving sustenance of God is coming in unexpected ways to nourish you and your family in the time of famine. While the world is in a state of unrest, you will remain at peace. In His presence, you will breathe again.

Kimberly Cabbagestalk is an anointed preacher, intercessor, and prophetic voice. She is the host of the *Arise Gathering*, an annual conference for women, and the founder of *Empowered Life Changers Ministries*, whose mission is to demonstrate the power of God and bring eternal change into territories by the ministry of the gospel. Kimberly has been the guest speaker for conferences, workshops, and special events.

She has traveled with evangelistic teams to share God's message of healing, liberation, and abundance.

In November 2018, she launched a women's network called *Buildhers*, through which she "inspires women to pioneer, create and innovate according to God's blueprints for their lives." She also expresses her creative abilities through her handmade jewelry boutique *Kimagisms*.

She acknowledged her call to ministry and preached her initial sermon in April 2001. She was licensed as a minister in 2003 and ordained in October 2007. She has served on the launch team for new ministries, sharing her expertise in implementing administrative processes and procedures. She has also served as Youth Pastor and Director of Evangelism and Outreach in her local church.

She is a graduate of National Bible College & Seminary, with a Bachelor of Biblical Studies. She is currently a student at Liberty University School of Divinity pursuing a Master of Arts in Religion (MAR). She has been employed at the Library of Congress in Washington, DC, for over 20 years. She is married to Willie Cabbagestalk, and together they have two beautiful daughters, Kyra Nicole and Kyliah Noelle.

Connect with Kimberly at:
www.empoweredlifechangers.org

Freedom isn't Free
Elizabeth Kampororo
Original Scribes Mobilize Member

◆

Freedom often has a high price tag with favorable results, whether immediate or not. Whether it is Jesus Christ suffering untold abuse and death to set His people free, brave African American's fighting for their inalienable rights as equal citizens, or a follower of Christ taking the narrow path, making the right decision is costly.

The subject of the poem is caught between two worlds, both of which demand full surrender. Initially, she makes a bad choice, never having been accepted and wanting to pay whatever deemed necessary to be well-liked by the "in-crowd."

As a believer in Jesus Christ, she has been called to renounce worldliness, her intense desire, and a pursuit leading to death. So, she elects to put her commitment to Jesus on hold. She then feels released to fight to earn the "privilege" of membership in the central, popular group of her peers. Even while she turns away from the Lord Jesus Christ, His loving voice continues to call her. The anticipated injury of returning to Jesus will involve complete abandonment of what she discovers is superficial allegiance.

The necessary action in either direction is pivotal; it is merely a question of which conflict she will take on. She remembers hearing that following Jesus yields abundant life. Ultimately, she makes Jesus her Lord, not her popular companions. She decides ongoing peace, which Jesus generously gives, is preferable to being included in the approved clique. She makes a better pledge.

Her struggle to maintain her faithfulness to her Lord will continue until the end of time. When she transitions from life on earth to eternal life with Jesus, the clash will end, and the wounds she sustained will heal.

◆ ◆ ◆

A battlefield
Broad and Bloody.
Deep wounds
Unseen
Unknown yet known
By those
Who have covered the same terrain.

On the outside looking in
Yearning
To join the insiders.
Willing to compromise

And quiet
The loving voice
Inside.
A battlefield
Of its own.

Choosing to leave
One fight for another.
The known
For the unknown.
Determined
Unyielding
Right instead of wrong
Holding fast
For the imminent
Victory.

A place
Of peace
Respite
Comfort calls
Nobody answers.

The battle continues.
There will be no end
Until the end.
Then,

Occupy

The laying down
Of arms.

Peace prevails.

The wounds
are healed.

◆   ◆   ◆

Elizabeth Kampororo is a bona fide free spirit, with an English degree and a passion for penning poems. She likes to tickle the reader's mind by creating a magnetic maze of suspense with surprising twists and turns. Coupled with writing poetry, Elizabeth runs her own online reading tutoring business, which combines her love for children and passion for teaching. In her free time, she loves to meet with friends, deliver endless scratches to her housemate's dog, and spark conversations that plumb the depths of a sea of varied topics. *Freedom Isn't Free* is her debut poem.

Connect with Elizabeth at:
TeacherElizabethK@hotmail.com

Break these Cords
Bernadine Okoro
Original Scribes Mobilize Member

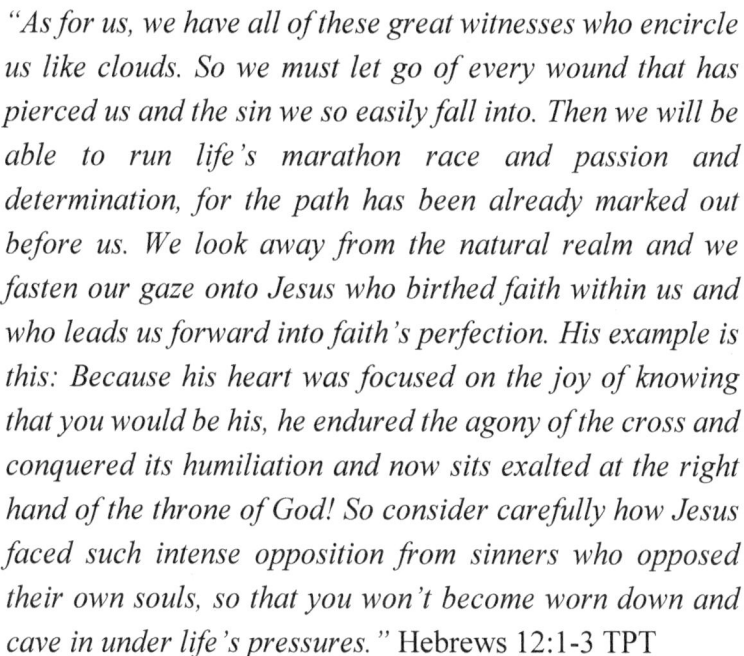

"As for us, we have all of these great witnesses who encircle us like clouds. So we must let go of every wound that has pierced us and the sin we so easily fall into. Then we will be able to run life's marathon race and passion and determination, for the path has been already marked out before us. We look away from the natural realm and we fasten our gaze onto Jesus who birthed faith within us and who leads us forward into faith's perfection. His example is this: Because his heart was focused on the joy of knowing that you would be his, he endured the agony of the cross and conquered its humiliation and now sits exalted at the right hand of the throne of God! So consider carefully how Jesus faced such intense opposition from sinners who opposed their own souls, so that you won't become worn down and cave in under life's pressures." **Hebrews 12:1-3 TPT**

I was well-acquainted with the word rejection. I pretty much embodied it. Lived with it. Slept with it. I ingested it. You could say it was one of my "womb" mates. Coming from a large family and being a twin, rejection seemed to be masked in ways I didn't understand as a child.

My parents immigrated to the United States in the 1970s. Home life was filled with African music, country music, and Igbo culture, traditions, and language. Traditional African expectations, gender roles, and patriarchal values often collided with Western society and its expectations, traditions, and values. As an inquisitive, docile, intelligent, and strong-willed young girl, the contradictions were glaring. Still, I instinctively understood the mantra that reigned over the household --- *"children should be seen and not heard."*

A series of childhood and adolescent events would eventually form the tapestry of experiences that seemed to solidify the notion that though I was smart, it wasn't enough. I was bullied almost every day from second grade to fifth grade. I experienced abrupt friendship breakups that left me devastated. Although I had friendships, it was ones that ended without warning that left an indelible mark in my soul. As middle school and high school came around, and relationships became more complex, it seemed easier to listen and be an ear than to share. The "school" boyfriends and extracurricular activities were a pleasant distraction from the duties that laid in wait in a house filled with brothers and sisters and the "African Press," which I secretly described as my mother.

The relationship between my mother and I was turbulent from the time I was eight to my early thirties. As a child, if there was a way to get her to notice me and give me credit for the extra chores I did when it wasn't my turn, I did it. I quickly saw the uneven distribution of responsibilities of grocery shopping, cooking, and cleaning handed to my twin sister and me while I perceived my older brother and younger sister and other siblings seemed to escape additional responsibilities. As a teenager, when I articulated and brought up these instances of favoritism and injustice, I encountered my mother's wrath, often being accused of things I didn't do. I sought her love, validation, and attention. I regularly walked on eggshells around her.

Since we didn't communicate feelings and emotions openly as a family, it suddenly became easy to overthink situations. I became very self-protective and fiercely independent. Emotionally, I didn't feel like I had anyone to rely on truly. I was a sensitive, methodical, and artistic teenager, but I decided in order to survive this phase in my life, I had to toughen up. Sensitivity had to go. Though I secretly proclaimed myself a "Daddy's girl," these combined external and internal relationship experiences birthed ideas, preconceptions, and thoughts that formed strongholds in my mind and heart. It would be the undercurrent of future relationships.

Years later, as a rededicated Christian, I found myself at the altar. The minister saw my brokenness and called it out. She spoke a word of knowledge saying, *"Second best, second-best... never good enough."* She declared the word of God over me. Tears of acknowledgment flooded my face confirming the years I struggled with the emotional pain and anguish. It was as if the spirit of rejection had mothered me while the spirit of abandonment fathered me. At the altar that day, as the minister prayed over me and laid her hands on me, the power of the Holy Spirit surged through me, and I fell to the floor. It was the first time that I had ever experienced the Holy Spirit's delivering power. I left service that day feeling refreshed, light, and happy. A weight I carried my whole life had finally been lifted. However, the feelings didn't last. More years passed before I fully understood the spiritual implications of what occurred during that fateful Sunday service.

Philippians 2:12 (KJV) says, *"Wherefore, my beloved, as ye have always obeyed, not as in my presence only, but now much more in my absence, work out your own salvation with fear and trembling."* As a rededicated Christian, I heard this scripture many times but never understood what it really meant. I knew I was delivered in my spirit. I began learning about renewing my mind. I rejoiced leaving church that day free from the demonic effects of rejection and abandonment only to return a few months later with those defeated feelings when circumstances hit. I was not liberated. I could not fully grow in my calling. I was saved, sanctified, and filled with the Holy Spirit, but I lived broken in many areas of my life. I often criticized myself, describing myself as an "intelligent mess." A shape-shifting masterpiece. My thoughts were broken. My perceptions, reasonings… tilted.

It was easier for me to depend on that which could be proven scientifically. I relied on my intellect more. I relied on what I could see and less on what I could sense. My instincts seemed to be off the charts when applied to creative endeavors, but they faltered everywhere else. I struggled to balance, leaning on my instincts and passions while using logic and reasoning. I fought in my attempts to distinguish between what makes sense and what makes faith. I certainly didn't trust people.

I overvalued the hurts and offenses. I dutifully tallied the wrongs done unto me while discounting the new wisdom and power growing inside me. I was impatient with myself and my process. Small beginnings preceded the smaller breakthroughs. My emotions at that time knew five ranges: anxiety, excitement, numbness, fear, or anger. So, I hid my emotions. I compartmentalized people, places, and things. I built an invisible fortress while serving God, work, home, and my church community. I secretly lugged around a knapsack full of painful memories and disappointments that grew bigger and bigger as I ventured out through life.

Recent conversations from a friend and mentor would help me unearth the lingering residue of limiting beliefs and negative thought patterns that kept me mentally bound to this vicious cycle. I would seek God for answers. When I got a prompting from the Holy Spirit, in pure excitement and relief, I would pursue the path towards righteousness. As I believed I was approaching the center of God's will for my life, an injustice or offense would train wreck me. There were debilitating cycles of paralyzing fear. Cycles of insecurities. Cycles of feeling misunderstood. Always feeling like I was on the outside looking in. Constantly feeling ignored or overlooked and, at times, invisible. Soon, cycles of loneliness gripped me so hard, I resorted to ungodly methods to cope. Perceptions seemed to turn into reality. I started busying myself with spiritual, intellectual, entrepreneurial, and artistic pursuits and endeavors. They were always my favorite go-to's. Busyness became my way to fill voids. When interests waned, I picked up new ones. I have always been curious, and I love novelty. But inwardly, I condemned my inability to follow through on my dreams or take advantage of opportunities. I couldn't carry out what God said to me, but I executed other people's visions with precision.

As my life and relationships expanded from my twenties to my thirties, then thirties to forties, so did my accomplishments, joys, misunderstandings, traumas, hurts, fears, and disappointments. The twisted cords of rejection and abandonment based beliefs had covertly filtered and controlled every aspect of my life. A 2017 job loss triggered a tsunami of old feelings and issues I thought I'd dealt with. I was caught in a mental and emotional tornado, right in the eye of the storm. When all of my attempts to find new work and reinvent myself failed, I sank into despair. I realized that I didn't have a healthy way of dealing with life's ups and downs. I passively managed change and transitions. My soul was crying out. My heart spilled out unresolved issues, and I needed to address them if I was going to move forward to the next level truly. By this point, I was bankrupt both mentally and emotionally. I found it difficult to make simple decisions. Unbelief and fear took residence in my heart. I still wanted to do God's will. I still wanted to fulfill my dreams. I still believed He called me. I wanted to walk in true dominion. I started my race, yet I stayed stagnant. I loved the Lord, yet my inner life needed revival. This breakdown would take me and my heart on a new journey. I needed help.

Have you ever faced a series of storms, a series of trials that seem to tear at the mental and emotional fabric of your identity? I have. In examining the losses within a four-year span: job loss, financial loss, relationship losses, death of loved ones, a parent's medical crisis, I found myself pressing the "pause" button on life, while it seemed everyone else moved forward; while the earth continued to spin on its axis. But why was this repeatedly my subconscious response?

What does abundant life look like? Could I still actualize more of my God-given dreams? Could I still execute His mandates? I desperately wanted the kind of peace and security that allows me to better journey through life's ups and downs. I wanted stronger, healthier, more reciprocal relationships. I wanted to know the covenant love that comes with a committed husband in marriage. How do I prosper in my soul? I have had to re-examine many situations through the lens of God's word. I have had to re-examine my mind, mainly, how I operated in perceived areas of defeat. I have had to submit to God doing the work He needs to do in the season He needs to do it and not resist Him or fight the process. I have had to take responsibility for my life and build my faith. I have had to learn and understand how to create "relationship intelligence." I am dealing with my soul, but now I am learning to do it with gentleness and patience. I have had to learn what self-care is and isn't. I continue to learn how to love myself, give love as well as receive love. So, the questions I probe myself with while in this process have been: Do I understand that my heart is leaking out issues? Will I allow God to do what He needs to do to grow me to maturity? What does patience and kindness to myself look like in God's healing process? What does it look like to trust the Holy Spirit?

God allows many difficult circumstances to occur in the lives of His people. What if these circumstances are used to train, develop, prepare, stretch, and mature His children? Jane Hamon, the author of "Discernment: The Essential Guide to Hearing the Voice of God," describes the heart as consisting of emotions, affections, desires, feelings, and passions. She also describes the mind as consisting of thoughts, intellect, reasonings, and perceptions.[2]

---

[2] Hamon, Jane (2019). Discernment: The Essential Guide to Hearing the Voice of God. Ada, MI, Baker Publishing Group

Imagine for a moment that God speaks to you saying, "Beloved, it is time…. It is time for you to do My will on this earth." You agree with this in your heart, and you know it. Years have come and gone. You grieve the "shoulda's-coulda's -woulda's." You sense the potential capacity of everything inside. You are a used vessel, yet, mentally, you continually share your documentary of "hurts," disqualifying yourself from God. Now imagine God is going to perform neurosurgery and heart surgery. He wants to align your thoughts, perceptions, and reasonings away from rejection and abandonment and towards His loving kindness. He wants to align your heart back to His heart.

He removes those diseased emotions, affections, desires, feelings, and passions. He gives you a blood transfusion. The blood of Jesus sanitizes, cleanses, and fills your heart. He binds up your wounds, then begins to work on your mind.

In this season, God is inviting you and me to come with Him to the Tent of Meeting. He wants us to break camp and move from this place of brokenness and double-mindedness and fully receive and operate in His love by faith. We have a decision to make. Will we break camp with these destructive cords, these patterns of negative perceptions, memories, emotions, and thoughts that no longer serve us? Are we willing to press our way to wholeness? What price are we willing to pay to be free here on earth finally?

We must break camp and move! Press our way through! Deal with the pain of the trauma. Deal with ourselves! Deal with the effects rejection and abandonment have had on our hearts and minds. We must consider seeking professional help if need be and come to the place that we will do whatever it takes. Isaiah 41:13 says, *"For I am the LORD your God who takes hold of your right hand and says to you, Do not fear; I will help you."(NIV)*

God will stay by our side. He will not go away-- even as we wrestle with our nature for the freedom and healing we desire. We must achieve that abundant life! Press through the pain...grief...loneliness. You see, the only way to break these cords and get to freedom is to PRESS!

If you are ready to move beyond your past, beyond the triggers, hang-ups, and limitations, pray this prayer in faith with me knowing that it is God's will for us to break these cords of bondage:

Father, I repent for my thoughts, feelings, and actions that have not been pleasing to you. I confess that I have unbelief, unforgiveness, fear, and rejection in my heart. I submit my heart, my soul, and my life to you now. Holy Spirit, strengthen me. Help me to work out my own salvation with fear and trembling, for I know that it is God who works in me both to will and to do for His good pleasure, according to Philippians 2:12-13. I thank you, Jesus, that you dwell in my heart. I decree and declare that I am being rooted and grounded in love now. I declare that I perceive the dimensions of Christ's love for me now by faith. I declare that I am filled with all the fullness of God, according to Ephesians 3:17-19. Holy Spirit, have your way in my heart, my soul, and in my life. I plead the blood of Jesus over my mind. As an act of my will, I move from this place of brokenness by faith, and I receive your love and the fullness right now, in Jesus' name. Amen.

For further reading and meditation: Revelation 21:7, Isaiah 54;10, Romans 12:1-2; Romans 5:3-5; James 1:12, James 1:2-4; 2 Corinthians 10:5

◆ ◆ ◆

Bernadine Okoro is a first-generation Nigerian-American writer, engineer, an award-winning educator, a voiceover talent and actress, documentary filmmaker, and information security professional.

She is the author of Peculiar Treasures, and co-author of Einstein Fellows: Best Practices in S.T.E.M. Education, 2nd Edition. She also voiced When Love Walked the Earth, a children's book by Eva Harley Chiphe. Bernadine has produced and directed two graduate film shorts and was a 2012 DC Community Heritage Project grant awardee with her documentary,

"Preserving Trinidad, Looking Through the Window of the Past; Opening the Door for the Future."

She holds a B.S. in Chemical in Engineering from Drexel University, an M.A. in Communications – Producing Film & Video and an M.A.T. in Secondary Education; both from American University.

Bernadine has been involved in ministry and the marketplace for over twenty years. She has served in various leadership capacities in the creative arts and Intercessory Prayer ministries; as well as Bridge Builders, a racial reconciliation ministry at her former church. She currently serves as one of the Intercessory Prayer leaders at her present church. She has worked as an engineer, is a veteran K-12 science teacher, and has been a youth mentor and Host home parent for several years. She is currently in Cybersecurity.

Bernadine believes in the power of using the creative arts and the word of God to impact the masses for Christ. She also believes in the power that safe communities can have in healing and transforming brokenness in relationships.

When not writing, Bernadine's interests span the gamut from personal development, to becoming a creative entrepreneur as well as being multilingual--- regaining Spanish fluency, learning Igbo, and Japanese. She resides in the metropolitan area of Washington, DC.

Connect with Bernadine at:
www.linkedin.com/in/bernadine-okoro

Occupy

Forward, March!

Marquita Everson

Special Guest

◆

Before I was born, the Commander in Chief (Yahweh) set me apart for a divine assignment in the earth. He provided me with the basic instruction manual for everyday living, which outlined the components of my spiritual armor and their specific use. Although I knew my mission and its relevance, I often lost sight of the intended goal as I traveled along this journey called life.

Where was my manual? Was my equipment functional, or was my issue a result of operator error? What was my objective again? Why was I lackadaisical, immobile, and unproductive? Could it be that I deviated from the Commander's divine plan, will, and purpose resulting from life happening? Maybe I was being led by my agenda, logic, reason, and ability because it seemed to be an easier and more practical way. When all the answers pointed to me and not to Christ, I realized I was spiritually asleep and marking time--marching in place without moving forward.

When the Commander in Chief, who chases, rescues, and saves those He loves, saw me in this halted and unsettled state, He allowed it to serve as a seed of discontentment for

Occupy

my current situation. This caused me to lean in very closely to hear His still small voice as He summoned me out of my slumber. He was gently urging me to arise and awaken so I could march forward into a greater revelation of knowledge, wisdom, and understanding. He was thoroughly equipping me to effectively Break Camp, Go-in, Go-to, and Occupy all that He called me to pursue.

◆　　　◆　　　◆

Legs up, feet down hitting the marching surface.
Running fast from my past with no intended purpose.
Complacency on the side of me yelling, **SLOW** down!
Stagnation in front of me shouting, I'm in the lead **NOW!**

Not moved. I'm ok with the pace that I am maintaining.
Not realizing that I'm losing more ground than I am actually gaining.
No urgency for the things God has said and is saying,
Or the call on my life that should have moved me to a posture of praying.

I'll get there when I get there is the attitude I displayed,
Directly resulting in many poor decisions I constantly made.

Trading the will of God for self-comfort led me astray,
Causing those assigned to me to experience needless delays.

Because I wouldn't: **B-R-E-A-K C-A-M-P!**

Now awakened to the error that was deeply anchored and rooted.
I was operating in disobedience and never even knew it.
Alert and attentive, better understanding who I am in Christ.
Life experiences have been learning tools to make me wise.

Knowing my worth and standing solid in my unique and special design.
An intimate relationship with the Father renders transformation in due time.
Saturating myself in the word and partnering with the Holy Spirit.
The enemy can try to employ his tactics, but this time, I'm not hearing it.

Embracing my assignment in the earth and moving in that direction.
Declaring and decreeing the victory in advance is my daily confession.

Occupy

Ready to deploy when The Great Commission is given.

Sharing the Good News and love of Jesus Christ for He has risen.

As I prepare to: **G-O T-O AND G-O I-N!**

On the journey, I must silence the many voices within.

If the enemy tried to derail me before, he will certainly do it again.

With my spiritual arsenal intact and on hand, I stand ready to engage.

Dispatching the heavenly hosts to help me -- the mighty Angel Brigade.

I am an heir; therefore, I have access to whatever belongs to my Father.

He's given me dominion over whatever I claim because I am His daughter.

Mediating on the word to discern the enemy's schemes and to utterly devour.

Casting down every demonic force through my inherited authority and power.

I am no longer operating in fear. I'm coming for you and your defeated crew.

I'm bussing in windows, knocking down doors as I charge straight through.

Taking responsibility for ALL that is set apart for me to manage and oversee.

Keeping my eyes on the prize, reaching the lost and setting the captive FREE.

When I: **O-C-C-U-P-Y!**

◆   ◆   ◆

Marquita L. Everson is a retired United States Army Master Sergeant. After honorably serving 20 years on active duty, she seamlessly transitioned into full-time ministry with Child Evangelism Fellowship of Central Texas, where she oversees a six-county region as the Local Director.

Her highest priority is sharing the Gospel with the next generation to help them discover, navigate, and press into their divine purpose.

Marquita has an aesthetic appreciation for poetry, and during her free time, she enjoys expressing her creativity and uniqueness through this notable art form. Additionally, fashion has always been the fabric of Marquita's essence.

She is known for her regal style and bold fashion statements and plans to use this gift to establish an upscale boutique that serves both men and women.

The delicately used apparel and accessories she deliberately searches for will aid in highlighting the treasure within each potential patron. She hopes that as she handles these special venues with careful stewardship, lives will be transformed, and people will be empowered to walk in self-worth, power, boldness, financial freedom, and healing.

Marquita is a native of Syracuse, New York, and resides in Killeen, Texas with her two sons, Malachi and Kae'Andre.

Connect with Marquita at:
Htboutique320@gmail.com

Barren and Pregnant with God's Love

Renee Joseph
Special Guest

◆

About four years ago, I had a hysterectomy. It was a necessary procedure because a fibroid was sitting on my lungs. According to the gynecologist, my uterus was the size of a woman seven months pregnant. Following the surgery, I experienced physical pain for about ten weeks. Yet, the emotional pain is ongoing.

What I am about to share with you is not to gain sympathy. I write this as a testimony and to share with other women dealing with a similar experience. I also write this as a form of therapy and healing for myself.

A few months after my surgery, tormenting thoughts flooded my mind and caused me to question my worth as a woman. To paint the picture, I think it is important to reveal my family genealogy here, or what little I know of it. I am an only child. My mother is the second eldest of eight children born to my grandmother. My grandmother was the third eldest of ten children born to my great grandmother. I am also the eldest grandchild. Most of my cousins have children except for two who have chosen not to have children. Can you imagine the weight of feeling as though you've broken the family lineage by not being able to have children of your own?

The reality of never being a mother hit me really hard around Mother's Day 2017. At that time, I was working as a Sales Associate at Burlington in Queens, New York. During my five-hour shift, I must have heard the words, "Happy Mother's Day," more times than I cared to. As hard as it was to hear that salutation repeatedly, it was seeing children hug and kiss their mothers that really broke me down. I was grieving deeply and didn't know how to express that outwardly. That's when I decided to start going to therapy at the Northport Veteran Hospital.

Within the African American community, some scoff at the idea of therapy and automatically assume, "you must be crazy." They sometimes even say, "you don't need a therapist; you should just pray about it." I am a prayer warrior, but after many painful months, I realized I needed more than prayer. I needed a therapist. I believe God gave us therapists for a reason, in the same way He gave us doctors. I believe my therapist was the vessel God used to help me release some things that were necessary for my healing process.

Unfortunately, I had to cancel my remaining therapy appointments after the fourth session. My mother was diagnosed with Stage IV breast cancer in 2016 and she was preparing for a mastectomy. After about nine months of chemotherapy, the doctor finally scheduled her surgery and she became my priority. I am happy to report that I recently started seeing a therapist again.

At times, I've questioned God. Yes, I said it. I questioned God. I asked Him why me? Why are less responsible, seemingly heartless people able to have children and not me? Am I not a loving, caring, God-fearing woman? I wish I could tell you what His answer was, but I never received one. Maybe I didn't sit still enough to hear his voice. I don't know. What I do know is that it irritates me when people say, "Oh, I'm sorry you can't have children, you can always adopt." Maybe they don't realize how their words sound to someone who cannot bear biological children, or perhaps they don't understand that adoption is not the solution for everyone. I wonder why someone would wish me a "Happy Mother's Day" every year knowing my situation? I wonder why some parents continuously post the latest pictures of their children on my Facebook page. While I understand they are proud parents, can they at least be sensitive to my feelings? But then again, maybe they don't know because I have never shared my grief with them.

How do I start such a conversation like this, especially with those who will never understand? That's when God revealed to me that I needed to start the conversation, which is one of the reasons I am sharing my testimony. Another reason is that I sometimes feel that within the body of Christ, childless women are ignored and overlooked. Churches and ministries don't traditionally reach out to those who have this issue and may still be grieving. But, with God's guidance, I believe my testimony will open doors to minister to women like myself within the church.

During a therapy session in 2016, God revealed that I have this abundance of love flowing on the inside that can be shared with a child, any child, who is not flesh of my flesh. Most recently, someone ministered to me and confirmed that very word from God. They say time heals all wounds. I've wondered when my time will come. But then, I look at the fourteen-inch scar on my stomach and feel the ache in my heart and have to remember that God is with me every step of the way. Because He is with me, I know that both the physical and emotional pain will eventually become bearable. This has been and continues to be a tremendous encouragement for me. I am confident that I am not alone and that one day, the motherly love I have inside will be poured out to the appointed ones.

◆ ◆ ◆

 Renee Joseph is a first-time author who has a heart for women who are hurting, women who have given up hope, and women who suffer in silence because they are ashamed to share their testimonies. She desires to see them healed, restored, and empowered.

She currently serves as one of the leaders for the Intercessory Prayer team at her church. She also enjoys discipling others through the church's 12 Week Discipleship Program and encouraging people with the truths of God's word.

Renee proudly served in the United States Marine Corps for 11 years. While on active duty, she earned her Master's Degree in Business Administration. Presently, she is employed as an Intake Coordinator at a non-profit organization that provides outreach, case management, and other core support to low-income Veteran families.

Renee is originally from Trinidad and Tobago. She currently resides in Long Island, New York.

Connect with Renee at:
josephrenee@hotmail.com

Occupy

The Body
Sade McAllister
Special Guest

◆

The Body was inspired by a vision the Lord gave me of a man going throughout the earth looking to unite his body. In the vision, I saw a partially assembled body stepping over seas, from continent to continent, with an agenda to gather the missing pieces. This reminded me of the imagery Billy Collins uses in his poem, *Purity*. In my view, the vision God gave me was a reverse process of the one seen in *Purity* because the man in Collins' poem was removing his skin and members for the evening. Whereas, in The Body, the man is assembling his body parts.

As I reflected on the condition of my own heart and the body of Christ, the Holy Spirit reminded me that it is not always a quick and easy task to unify us as one, well-functioning body. The Holy Spirit also revealed those things that cause us to reject and fight the process.

I have experienced some trauma and exposure to less than godly environments, which opened doors for resentment, envy, bitterness, low self-worth, depression, shame, and rejection or feeling as if I'm merely tolerated as opposed to truly loved by those around me. I've felt (both as a child and an adult) like no one would listen if I spoke, no one wants to be around me, no one would be bothered if I was no longer around, or they'd get over it quickly when compared with the other people in their lives. I'm painfully familiar with the feeling of being a bother or a burden or an irritant to people. I've believed so many lies that people and the enemy have presented to me about life, myself, and people. All these things gave way to shame and offense, which caused me to hide away, distance myself from people, and reject the process of unifying with the body of Christ.

So I got to thinking, what would the process look like personified and also, how does it affect the Kingdom of God when we allow these hindrances to beat us and separate us from our vital roles in the body? Well, it is my understanding that when the Lord calls us to occupy, He did not mean for occupying to be a spectator sport. Occupy is a verb that is not stagnant but takes hold of the authority given and gets things done. If our hands and legs, in envy, are unwilling to work together with the head, how can the body work the land? The thing is, the unification of some parts and not all parts are not effective. We have to work to resolve the discrepancies that keep us out of the will of God so that we can unify to fulfill the purpose of God and occupy until He comes.

◆ ◆ ◆

A man wrote about a man
who, coming home to rest,
removes his skin
and all its fleshly parts.

Maybe
the night before,
after he finishes scribbling his heart out,
he even dismantles the bones.

I imagine so.

Maybe
when he wakes
he first seeks his head.
Finding it, he is well pleased.

The neck,
feeling insecure,
rejected,
hides himself from the man.

Precious time wasted,
the neck is soon retrieved
and that man
is well pleased.

Shoulders, backbone, and abdomen
understand the process.
Lined up and ready,
they take their places.

That man is well pleased.

Occupy

Now,
the right arm envies the left.
The left-hand envies the right.
All fingers,
but the left ring finger
feel overworked
and underappreciated.
In a quarrel
an hour is lost.

Finally, twin wrists
bring peace amongst the brothers
and they all fall into position.
With every one of them,
that man is well pleased.

It is noon.

The rest of the body,
one member after another,
connects and joins
to the body of that man
and he is well pleased.

It is now 5.

Nearly dark.
That man missed work.
That man has nothing left to do,
but *"remove [his] flesh,
and hang it over a chair"*,[3]

---

[3] Collins, B. (1991). *Questions about angels: Poems* (p. 41). Pittsburg, PA: University of Pittsburgh Press.

become one with his nakedness
and write before he rests.

With lessons learned
and the idea
that they'll do better tomorrow
that man is well pleased.

◆   ◆   ◆

Sade L. McAllister is a first-time author who began writing poetry and other creative works at the age of eight and creating visual arts in junior high school. From fourth grade through college, her church's youth leader, Amber Johnson, her language arts teacher, Mrs. Stacy Corcoran Bryan, and other literary and visual arts teachers encouraged Sade to read, write, draw and paint. They also aided in developing her ability to articulate some of her internalized struggles through these various art mediums. This nurture not only inspired Sade to continue in creative expressions, but also fostered in her a desire to teach and equip other hurting young ladies to use some of the same tools that were given to her to successfully combat their issues.

Presently, Sade volunteers as a teacher with Child Evangelism Fellowship's Good News Club program sharing the Gospel of Jesus Christ with elementary school children. She also channels her love of writing and enabling other writers by creating hand-bound journals.

Connect with Sade at:
kingdomkupboards@gmail.com

Redemptive Reflections: Career

Dianna Davis-Small

Scribes Mobilize Member

◆

"We can make our plans, but the Lord determines our steps."
Proverbs 16:9 NLT

I've read several books on chronos and kairos time and listened to multiple teachings about both. Yet, my personal experience with God has taught me that no matter when I believe things should occur in my life, they will happen according to His timetable and not mine. So, it is from this humbled position that I share some redemptive reflections from my God designed 27-year career.

In June 1993, I graduated from Lewis University with a Bachelor of Science in Aviation Administration. I desperately wanted to work for an airline, but jobs were scarce due to the economy. I didn't let this seeming roadblock stop me, though. Instead, I decided to apply for a position with the Chicago Department of Aviation, Airport Operations Division at O'Hare International Airport. When I arrived at City Hall to submit my application, I found an '*X*' and the words "*closed*" on the bulletin board.

However, next to it was a job announcement for an Aviation Communications Operator (ACO). My eyes honed in on the word *"aviation,"* and I was compelled to apply.

I was selected for an interview during which the hiring official bluntly asked why I wanted a job that was not associated with the airlines. I said, *"Ma'am, I want the job because I want to be as close to aviation as possible."* In my mind, getting my foot in the door by working for the Department of Aviation would be a good start. A few weeks later, the hiring manager called to let me know I was selected for the position and that of all the people selected, I had the least experience but was the most passionate. I probably was most excited about being hired too.

Reflection: Sometimes, passion can trump experience. As a new graduate, your education may be the only qualifier if your degree is in the field you apply for. But, if you don't have the experience, think outside of the box. Apply for jobs that may not directly match your degree but can grant you access to the field you prefer. Then go for it!!

I recall my training like it was yesterday. I learned the layout of Chicago O'Hare International Airport (terminals and the airfield). For me, the terminal and airlines related to airline operations while airfield related to airport operations; all things I studied while earning my Aviation Administration degree. The Communications Center had four consoles—

Access Control, Fire, Police, and Security. Each console required in-depth training and terminology comprehension for dispatching personnel to events on and off the airport. I needed to know the airport like the back of my hand.

During a particular shift briefing, management told us to be on guard because the Federal Aviation Administration (FAA) would be running tests that week. While manning the Access Control console, someone rang the intercom and said they'd left their identification at home. They asked me to let them through the door. I declined their request and told them they would have to get their ID or someone with the proper access to escort them. Later that day, the FAA Security Manager told me we passed the test. I seized the moment to ask questions. I told him I had a degree in Aviation Administration, which broadly touched on everything related to the Aviation Field but not FAA Civil Aviation Security. I went on to ask him if they were hiring and was informed that there was still a hiring freeze. He said he would let me know when it was lifted, and he would personally bring me an application. He kept his word and did just that. I applied for a Civil Aviation Security Inspector position, and to my dismay, I did not make the best-qualified list.

I continued to work as an ACO for about 18 months and eventually became an Airport Operations Supervisor (AOS). This was the job I originally went to City Hall to apply for and found the announcement closed. As an AOS, I supervised airport openings and closings and ensured taxiways and runways were clear of debris. I escorted construction and maintenance workers onto the airfield and monitored their work. I also became a responder to the same incidents I once dispatched others to.

In the summer of 1996, on a Friday, to be exact, my father called me at work to tell me someone from the FAA called about a job. When I returned the call, I was asked if I was still interested in the Civil Aviation Security Inspector position. This was the position I wasn't previously qualified for. I was flabbergasted but quickly opened my mouth to say "yes." I was interviewed and subsequently offered the job. I was told I would have to move to Indianapolis, Indiana, and would be the first African American working in this office. Prior to this offer, I had a desire to move out of state but ironically, I no longer had the urge to do so. I accepted the offer and was excited about such a great opportunity. I took a $10,000 pay cut to join the federal government. I considered it a strategic move because, in two years, I would surpass the pay I made as an AOS, and in 3-years would nearly double that pay.

Reflection: Be ready at all times to seize the moment. Delayed doesn't necessarily mean denied. You may have to take a seeming step back to leap forward.

My first airline inspection was exhilarating. My supervisor and I arrived at Indianapolis International Airport only to find the plane we were slated to inspect would be leaving shortly. Per the Official Airline Guide (OAG), we thought we had ample time for the inspection. At that time, the OAG was how people checked flight arrivals and departures before doing so on the internet. I ran to the plane to interview the pilot and complete my portion of the airline inspection. The flight took off as scheduled and without incident. This inspection is significant in my career development because it helped me understand how important my job was and demonstrated my commitment to ensuring the airport and airline were successful.

I worked with amazing and dedicated professionals who took me under their wings, mentored, and coached me to be an excellent inspector. I gained significant experience as a young inspector/special agent, worked air shows, and participated in many airport and airline inspections. I also conducted inspections for FAA government facilities such as Air Route Traffic Control Towers. I had an awesome time at the Indianapolis office. My time there ended in 1998 when my father passed away, and I moved back to Chicago. I took an agent position in the Chicago FAA Civil Aviation Security Field Office and eventually became the lead agent at the Chicago Midway International Airport.

On September 11, 2001, I happened to be conducting an airline test. I was an undercover agent dressed as a passenger. I broke cover after word spread like wildfire throughout the airport that the twin towers in New York City had been hit. I worked with the airport authority to shut the airport down. As you can imagine, it was all hands on deck throughout the FAA to address this national emergency.

A few months later, I was assigned to an Operations Center detail in Washington, DC. As soon as I stepped into the center, my mind instantly went back to my position as an ACO at the O'Hare Communications Center. It was dark, it housed several monitors and consoles, and there was a lot of action. Yet, this time, I was a Federal employee with eight years of experience, and I was ready to take on my part in the war against terrorism.

During my detail in Washington, DC, my hotel room happened to be near the side of the Pentagon hit by American Airlines Flight 77. One late night, while gazing out of the window, the Lord spoke to me and told me I'd be coming back to live there. Before the detail ended, the FAA Administrator permanently placed the Operations Center into effect for 24/7/365 days a year. This prompted me to apply to be a watch officer. One door was closing and another door was opening that would lead me to a call to action at a federal operations center.

From August 2001 to August 2002, I was also in the Graduate School, United States Department of Agriculture,

Executive Leadership Program (ELP). The ELP was a development program that provided leadership and managerial training and development opportunities for mid-level Federal employees preparing for future leadership positions. This was the first time I began to desire a Senior Executive Service (SES) position. I completed a 60-day detail assignment at the National Transportation Safety Board in Washington, DC. I completed a 60-day detail assignment at the National Transportation Safety Board in Washington, DC. I also completed a 30-day assignment at the Federal Emergency Management Agency (FEMA) in Chicago before moving to the DC area as a J-Band (GS-14 equivalent) Team Lead Watch Officer in July 2002. This position allowed me to take on new challenges. I supervised individuals who were my senior and those with different experience levels. In 2003, I was promoted to a K-Band as a Supervisory Transportation Security Specialist and my pay more than quadrupled.

Reflection: A closed door can lead you to the right door and subsequent opportunities that push you towards purpose.

In 2004, I began applying for Master's programs paid for by the government. After about four years and four denials, I was just about to give up. One day, I saw an email for an opportunity to attend the National Defense University, a Department of Defense college. I almost missed the application deadline. But thankfully, I was able to submit it on time. I specifically applied for the Industrial College of Armed Forces (ICAF) at Fort McNair in Washington, DC. I thought applying for this would increase my chances of acceptance. It was the type of program for which the government would only have to cover my tuition and not tuition, room, and board and per diem like other programs. Although I was accepted, my acceptance was for another program. The review panel felt I was a better candidate for the Joint Forces Staff College, Joint Advanced Warfighting School (JAWS), in Norfolk, Virginia.

When the program official called me, I was out for a walk. She said, *"I have good news and bad news, which do you want first?"* I asked for the good news. She said, *"the good news is, we would like to accept you into the program, however the bad news is, you only applied for ICAF."* She asked if I was able to travel? I told her, yes. A few weeks later, my mother, who had moved to the area with me, and I drove to the college to check things out. As we were driving, it dawned on me that I was going away to college as a full-time student, an opportunity I'd always wanted.

Reflection: God doesn't need your help. At the appointed time, He will bless you in ways you cannot even imagine.

Out of a class of 42 students, I was one of three African Americans and one of three women. I visited the library every day after class and practically stayed until it closed. This was a dream come true for someone bookish like me and who loves to learn. I even missed a family reunion to remain in school and study. I would study all weekend long, only to go to class on Monday and not be able to answer any homework or reading assignment questions posed by the instructor.

Within a month of my birthday, September 2, 2008, to be exact, I came home from class and took a nap. I awoke with shortness of breath and erratic heartbeats. This had been going on for about a month. I knew I wouldn't make it to my 38th birthday if I didn't get checked out. I drove to the emergency room and underwent several tests to find out I was under a lot of stress, which I was not handling well. The visit went something like this:

> *"Ma'am, we can't find anything wrong with you. Are you under any stress?"*
>
> *"I'm in an 11-month Master's Degree program at a military planning school, and I don't know anything about the military or planning, and I have to write an Operations Plan, thesis and defend my thesis to graduate." (with the effect of a run-on sentence)*
>
> *"Ma'am, you're going to have to find a way to manage your stress. Perhaps yoga or working out, detox, or something, but stress is causing the erratic heartbeats and shortness of breath."*

"Ok. Will do."

I was in shock. This could not be happening to Dianna from Chi-town. That cool motorcycle riding girl who beat men all day long racing up and down dem streets in the Chi on Lake Shore Drive. Not Dianna, that inquisitive inspector who could inspect airports and air carriers all day long and find something wrong when others couldn't. Not Dianna, who worked airport security breaches, diverted aircraft, briefed Agency heads, and led high-level national strategic working groups. Naw, that couldn't be the case. You see, I was the one who always knew what to do, and I was the one who led others. For the first time in my entire life, I was as clueless and inexperienced as I'd ever been, and I had to totally depend on God.

I began managing the stress. I took up yoga as suggested. I signed up for a gym membership, which had a sauna. I continued visiting the library every day, and some of my classmates even started tutoring me. I was serious about completing this program. It truly was the hardest thing I'd intellectually encountered in my life, and for the first time, I was not as comfortable being the minority as I had been since college. I'm always aware of being the minority but was never bothered by it because I excelled in every job I had. Now, I truly felt vulnerable and as if God had played a trick on me. I was in a foreign place and learning a foreign language (military planning) with nothing to make me stand out except my skin color. I was intimidated. Everyone around me looked the same and spoke the same because some of them had been to war and even served under high-ranking generals. I didn't have the same experiences as my classmates, yet I had to demonstrate an understanding of military operations and planning and write a thesis to graduate. Not to mention, the government was paying for this opportunity. This was tough. I literally felt like all eyes were on me and that I had to prove myself even more so than the others.

I ended up finding a spiritual parallel that helped me navigate through the program. I reflected on what I learned during a 7-month Prayer Warrior Training class I graduated from in September 2001. Ephesians 6:12 explains this parallel:

> *"We're not waging war against enemies of flesh and blood alone. No, this fight is against tyrants, against authorities, against supernatural powers and demon princes that slither in the darkness of this world, and against wicked spiritual armies that lurk about in heavenly places." (The Voice)*

The Prayer Warrior training prepared me as a prayer warrior/intercessor to identify my spiritual gifts, callings, assignments, and purpose and to use my spiritual authority to advance in spiritual warfare against the enemy. In-kind, the Joint Advance Warfighting School helped me to be an effective operational and strategic planner. I gained critical analysis skills specific to the application of all aspects of national power across the full range of military operations, and I learned to develop plans for warfighters with those skills. God and that experience were all I had to draw upon. Eventually, I completed the program and graduated with a Master's of Science in Joint Campaign Planning and Strategy.

Reflection: Remember to let go and let God. Relax. Be confident in knowing God is in control even when you don't have all of the details.

A year after graduating, I returned to my position of record. I knew that if I didn't use the planning skills I gained, I would quickly lose them. Most military graduates fulfill their joint professional education and are promoted. Civilians do not follow the same track. Therefore, I began seeking jobs that required planning skills. Within six months, I landed a job as a Transportation Security Specialist (Planner) at the Transportation Security Administration Headquarters. It was a newly created position for which both my aviation and planning experience was vital.

Reflection: Experience in life is not linear. Look for the spiritual and natural connection of things in life and be mindful that you never know what type of experience will prepare you for the next.

As mentioned previously, in 2003 I achieved K-Band status, but in 2013 I was downgraded to J-Band level again due to new stipulations for supervisory K-Band requirements. This made me feel as if I was regressing because it came with an unexpected cost. The previous lateral move from a Supervisory K-Band to a Technical K-Band as a Planner resulted in the downgrade. Nevertheless, I continued to look for opportunities to grow and advance in my career.

In 2017, I was presented with an excellent opportunity to attend a five-week leadership program through the TSA Leadership Institute, School of Senior Leadership Studies. This program was facilitated by the faculty from American University's Key Executive Leadership Program. Some of the teaching was based on Nick Craig's book, "Leading from Purpose". The process of developing a Higher Purpose statement is where I began to pivot. The main point of the exercise was not just about moving up the career ladder, but it was about developing a compass to direct a path to defining what was really important—living in purpose. In his book, Nick Craig stated, *"The statement is just words and our purpose is much more than words. The words are like a key that unlocks a door. The key by itself, like a purpose statement, has no value. It's the room we access because of the key that matters, the purpose that has always been leading us."* [4]

---

[4] Craig, N. (2018). *Leading with Purpose.* The Hatchette Book Group, Inc.

To step into the room of purpose and live a purposeful life, I followed a process adapted from Nick Craig's book that consisted of deep self-reflection on (1) magical moments of my childhood; (2) the most challenging experiences in my life—crucibles. Crucibles are experiences that shape leaders such as a trial and test, a point of deep self-reflection that forces leaders to question who they are and what matters to them, and (3) a passion that has fueled me over time.

After completing this four-month process of self-reflection, I emerged more determined and confident as defined in my purpose statement:

DIANNA – Fearless Pilot and Rough Rider you can count on.

This statement centers me because I wanted to be a pilot from a young age. I contribute this to yearly trips with my father to Los Angeles, California, which became the birthplace of my love for airplanes. A pilot has to file a flight plan, stay the course, and land the aircraft. The rough rider in me is daring, confident, and willing to take risks. Yet in both, I am a devoted person whom people can always count on. Even though I did not become a pilot as a profession, and I no longer ride motorcycles, I still identify with both because they cause me to operate and lead from a place of strength.

Reflection: It is not a title, career, or money that defines you but that which is on the inside of you—your purpose.

I began writing this piece with great hope that I would finally be selected for the Department of Homeland SES Candidate Development Program (CDP). Once again, I didn't make the cut. I subsequently applied for a position I truly believed God prepared me for over the course of my career. I thought, *"Yes Lord, in this year of redemption, some of my goals will come to pass.* Unfortunately, I wasn't even selected for an interview. Amid disappointment and great frustration, I thought, *"so, now what? Now, I dig deep, remain true to my convictions, and maintain my devotion to helping others achieve excellence."*

While I may not have made the impact I imagined, I believe God has used me to make an impact according to His intent for my life. He's used my gifts and talents in multiple ways. Some have been specific to work, such as, leading the development of TSA's first-ever Diversity Strategic Plan; and serving as a mentor both formally and informally in the office. Others have been non-work specific such as being in the right place at the right time in the office to pray for or be a comfort to colleagues and friends.

Sometimes people get delivered from a situation, and sometimes they get delivered while still in the situation. In my case, I have been delivered while still in a situation. In the last ten years, I applied for eight SES CDP programs, and in the past five years, I applied for eight jobs to no avail. It has been discouraging, but one thing I've come out knowing is that God's will shall be done.

Reflection: Having the right mindset during tests or trials is essential. It's not how fast you come out but how strong you come out. Despite the weariness waiting can sometimes bring, it produces benefits and characteristics such as patience and compassion that may not be gained otherwise.

A good scripture to sum up this piece is *"A person may have many ideas concerning God's plan for his life, but only the designs of his purpose will succeed in the end." Proverbs 19:21* TPT

As Dottie Peoples sings, *He may not come when you want Him, but He'll be there right on time. I'll tell you He's an on-time God. Yes, He is."*[5]

Father, I pray for the people who are reading and will read this book. May they place their hope and confidence in You; and that they are prosperous and blessed as a result.

---

[5] Peoples, D (1994). On Time God [Song]. On Dottie Peoples & the People's Choice Chorale [Album]. Gospel AIR Records & Tapes.

I also decree and declare that they:

- Develop knowledge, skills, and abilities that are transferable and will be diligent about applying them in meaningful ways.

- Make strategic moves that advance them in their career.

- Be resilient and regain any emotional territory lost due to any career setbacks.

- Will not be weary in well-doing; for in due season they shall reap if they faint not (Galatians 6:9).

- Gain access to influential people, and the right gift, presented at the right time, opens new opportunities for them (Proverbs 18:16).

In Jesus' Name. Amen.

Dianna Davis-Small is a shrewd professional with over 27 years of progressive leadership and public servant experience. She's garnered skills in multiple aviation disciplines, including aviation communications, aviation security inspections, and investigations; airport operations; crisis management; policy coordination; project management; and strategic planning. She has been employed with the Transportation Security Administration since its inception and proudly serves the agency with institutional knowledge.

Dianna holds a Bachelor's of Science in Aviation Administration and a Master's of Science in Joint Campaign Planning and Strategy. She is also a graduate of the TSA Leadership Institute, School of Senior Leadership Studies, and the USDA Executive Leadership Development Program.

She is the founder and Chief Executive Officer of Freeman Ventures LLC, a small business specializing in a range of planning services. She and her husband own Kool Kids Icecream, an ice cream truck business. Dianna also serves the community through her board of directors' seat on the Fort Washington Estates Civic Association. Moreover, she is a Communications Director for Helpmate for Hope, a non-profit organization in Los, Angeles, California.

In addition to her professional and business experience, Dianna has over 20 years of experience in ministry. She is an evangelist and proven servant-leader, having served as church secretary and in evangelism, intercessory prayer, mentee-mentor ministry, missionary ministry, teaching, preaching, outreach, leadership, choir, and praise team.

Dianna's determination to continue pursuing a senior leadership position in government despite the no's is very inspiring. Her goal is to help people see that persistence is succeeding. She offers reflections of her career to inspire hope in the midst of longsuffering and to stay the course. Dianna is a first-time author and looks forward to publishing similar and other content in the future.

Dianna resides in Fort Washington, Maryland with her husband, Robert.

Connect with Dianna at:
hfreemanventuresllc@gmail.com

Occupy

Possess the Land
Tanya Stephenson
Special Guest

◆

I woke up from a dream that made me question my future. From what I could remember, it was about me owning my own home in my name with no cosigner. I questioned my future because it had been a rough couple of years financially. I was recently divorced and just gaining my footing with paying bills on time. That's when the four-letter word came creeping in like a thief at night. You know the word I am talking about, *FEAR*.

At first, I thought, "no way," because, at the time, I was renting a home with three bedrooms and 2.5 baths. I felt lucky for being able to afford to live there. I ignored the dream … I ignored the notion of me owning my own home… I ignored being able to do something like that by myself. The negative thoughts ravaged my mind. What if I cannot keep it up… what if I can't keep it… what if I cannot afford it? So, I did what any fearful person in my position would probably do; I kept it moving.

It was not until the owner of the house I'd been renting for three years called me. He told me he was entertaining the idea of selling his home, and he wanted to give me an opportunity to purchase it. At the time, I had already put the notion of owning my own home out of my head and still believed I wouldn't be able to take that type of financial leap. Now keep in mind, I enjoyed living in his home, and it taught me great lessons on what to expect when owning my own but I didn't feel like it was my *home*. Yet, I entertained the idea because it was easy. I would not have to move; I'd be able to stay in the same school zone, which meant my children wouldn't have to change schools. Not to mention, I liked the neighborhood. It seemed like a win-win situation.

I continued entertaining the idea, but it wasn't until I spoke to a close friend that made this statement that I began to believe it could happen. My friend said, *"He made you a promise, and came to you in your dream. He wants you to go and get it. Don't ignore what He has set up for you."* As I listened, I began to gain confidence and started preparing myself for this new endeavor.

I found a realtor, explained my situation, and we began the home buying process. I was pre-approved for $180,000.

In this day and time, there is not much you can buy with that amount. I was positive but not at first. Feelings of not getting what I wanted, a four-bedroom, two-car garage, and a big backyard, slowly began to fade away. I spoke with the owner, and he advised me that he would be putting the home on the market for $250,000. As you can imagine, I was taken aback because my first thought was the house is not worth that amount. His response also convinced me that the house was not for my family and me. I never told the owner what I was approved for, so I advised him that I would think on the matter and return to him in a week.

Six weeks before my lease ended, I decided I was not going to buy the home from the owner, and I started aggressively looking at other homes in the area. A moment of doubt came into my mind during this time, but then I focused on my friend, reminding me that "the land" was promised to me, and it was my job to occupy the land. Putting things in perspective, I had to remind myself that the amount I was approved for shouldn't be the focus. The focus was going after what was promised, which was the house God decided was for me and mine. I started looking for homes and didn't pay attention to the cost (within reason). The realtor set up appointments, and we viewed what I felt would suit my family.

The saying "When you know, you know" is so true! A home I drove by every day had a for sale sign in the front yard for almost eight months. I never stopped to find out what the selling price was. One day, I stopped by the house, grabbed a flyer, and called the number to ask about the asking price. Once I spoke with the realtor, and she quoted the price, I was prompted to go to the bank to find out what they could do for me. The next day I went to my bank, and within an hour, the bank pre-approved me for a more considerable amount, but that amount still wasn't enough to purchase the home. Although disappointing, I kept looking for a home with my new pre-approved amount, which increased my options. The problem was, I really liked the house I drove by every day. It was something about the house that just drew me to it.

About two weeks later, my realtor called and said the sale price decreased a whole 30,000 dollars, which brought the price point right where I needed it to be to make the purchase and to secure the desired mortgage payment. I jumped on the deal and put an offer on the house. Keep in mind; I hadn't viewed the house yet. I was moved based on a gut feeling and nothing else. My realtor made the offer and simultaneously scheduled a viewing.

On the day of the viewing, as soon as I walked in, I said to myself, "this is it." When I walked upstairs, I yelled out, "This is it!" When I stepped into the backyard, I yelled, "this is it." It was as if the house was waiting for my family and me. To sum it all up, I was the only one to put an offer on the house. The owner accepted my offer with equity already in the property! I moved two days before my lease ended, and I have occupied the land ever since. It was time to move; I didn't allow seeming setbacks to hinder me, I kept moving forward, and in doing so, my family and I walked into the land God secured for us. This experience redefined my faith and trust in the Lord!

◆ ◆ ◆

Tanya Stephenson is a Washington, DC native by way of suburban life in Lanham, Maryland. She is a member of Sigma Gamma Rho Sorority, Incorporated, and the local Life Journeys Writer Guild in Waldorf, Maryland. A graduate of Strayer University, she possesses a Master of Business Administration in Computer Networking and a Master of Public Administration. Despite her academic achievements, she found her calling in graphic design and visual communication. Using her creativity, she has been able to successfully convey her customers' passion visually through vibrant business logos, unique business cards, and captivating book covers and websites for local small businesses.

In 2018, she took a leap of faith and founded Compassionate Designs LLC, a graphic design company. She embodies the meaning of the word compassionate (feeling concern for others) in every project she undertakes. She invests her time and energy into understanding her customers, embeds their essence into the project, brings their thoughts into reality, and, most importantly, alleviates the burden of navigating how to visualize their brand.

Soon after founding Compassionate Designs LLC, Tanya again answered the call of her entrepreneurial spirit, founding Compassionate Designs Publishing. This venture began with inspiration from a close friend and author who sought to help other authors achieve their dreams of publishing their work without the exorbitant costs associated with well-connected publishing companies. Compassionate Designs Publishing aims to assist aspiring authors with publishing services that fit their budgets.

Tanya's motto is, *"there is a book in everyone; make time to write it out and publish it."*

She is grateful for her three amazing kids who help her remain grounded, reminding her that anything is possible with hard work and determination.

Connect with Tanya at:
www.compassionatedesigns.com

Breakthrough and Overcome
LaShaun O'Bryant
Original Scribes Mobilize Member

We are not called to live a defeated life! Jesus came to redeem us from the curse of the law and for us to accept our inheritance in addition to our power to breakthrough and overcome. Every day we battle with our mistakes and the overall difficulties of life. They enslave our minds with guilt, shame, and condemnation. God does not intend for us to be bound. What we think bears fruit, so we cannot walk in doubt or move in fear if we want to live in victory.

Faith overshadows fear, but faith can't work unless we acknowledge God's promises and believe His word. No transformation or change is permanent if we do not renew our mind continuously.

We have to decide whether we want to continue holding on to the things that bind us up or if we want to be delivered. 1 John 5:4-5 (NIV) tells us that; *"for everyone born of God overcomes the world. This is the victory that has overcome the world, even our faith. Who is it that overcomes the world? Only the one who believes that Jesus is the Son of God."*

We are the righteousness of God in Christ. Only by the Spirit of God are we able to OVERCOME in this life. The power and grace of God transforms our opinions, impressions, feelings, and brokenness, and He shapes us into suitable vessels for His use. We must come into agreement with what He says about us and believe that He wants to establish a passionate purpose in us to accomplish His mission and will. We have to also remember that there is nothing we've done or thought that He won't forgive us for. We are loved by God and every day is a miracle given to us to thrive, breakthrough and overcome.

As you partner with heaven, my prayer is that:

- You repent for your sins and give your heart to God

- You are convinced of your authority and identity in Jesus Christ.

- God's love overtakes you and that His favor and peace floods your life.

- The Lord gives you wisdom and discernment to properly confront and deal with every area in your life that is oppressed, possessed or controlled by anyone and anything outside of Him.

- The fire of God heals your brokenness and that He uses every hurt and disappointment for His Glory.

I also decree and declare that:

- You are Royalty! You are a child of the living God, a kingdom citizen, joint-heir with Christ.

- No weapon formed against you shall prosper because you are an overcomer.

- You've overcome your sinful nature and the lies of the enemy about who you are.

- Every evil spoken over your life, your family, your finances, your health, your relationships, and your destiny, are terminated.

- God is your refuge and strength in the time of trouble.

- No one and nothing can snatch you out of God's hand.

- Self-hate, bitterness, depression, shame, and guilt be destroyed in your life.

- Yokes are broken, and chains fall off that have held you captive.

- You are who God says you are.

- The spirit of peace and joy abounds in your life.

- You are loved, fearless, relentless, and equipped with Kingdom authority to BREAKTHROUGH, OVERCOME and live an abundant life!

In Jesus' name!

◆ ◆ ◆

LaShaun O'Bryant is a woman of God on a mission to save souls. She speaks the truth and believes in the promises of God. She believes in praying, fasting, and teaching others at every opportunity. She also believes God wants to prosper, heal, deliver, and mature women to be His warriors. She's determined to be a light that impacts and guides others to our Beloved King Jesus.

Her ministry experience is vast. She's worked with adults and youth in varying capacities. She established Daughters by Design, a ministry for young women, at a church she previously attended. In 2011, she co-founded "Sisters with Purpose Kingdom of Heaven Ministries" (SWPKOH). SWPKOH is a non-profit (501c3) ministry without walls.

SWPKOH hosts several events and community outreaches throughout the year as a means to share the word of God with others. Some of the most recognizable SWPKOH events are the annual women's retreat held at the beautiful Sandy Cove Retreat Center in North East Maryland, monthly women's bible study, chit-chats, mid-day lunches. During these times of intimate fellowship, the Gospel is shared with "sister-girlfriends" who get real, share common life issues, and are encouraged in a safe and fun environment.

LaShaun is also connected to and partners with several ministries in the community that serve the same purpose as SWPKOH -- building the Kingdom of God. She has been actively involved in prison ministry for several years. Her influence and inspiration paved the way to a membership on the Kairos International Ministry Advisory Council, where she held several positions to include Vice President and spiritual director. As a member and officer of the organization, she came to understand better the circumstances that impact women in prison and in the community. This knowledge positioned her to reach more women in and outside of prison walls and equipped her to help create and improve services for them.

In addition to her ministry experience, LaShaun has been a Federal Government employee for over 25 years.

LaShaun has been happily married to George F. O'Bryant, Jr. for thirty years and is the mother of Sham'mah Gabriel

O'Bryant, a 2018 high school graduate whom she homeschooled and is grooming to be an entrepreneur.

Connect with LaShaun at:
prepare2prosper@comcast.net

Occupying the Spheres of Ministry and the Marketplace

Bernard Boulton
Special Guest

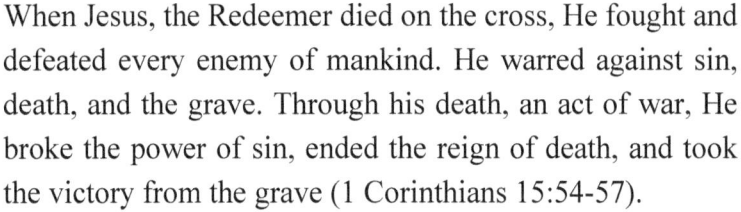

When Jesus, the Redeemer died on the cross, He fought and defeated every enemy of mankind. He warred against sin, death, and the grave. Through his death, an act of war, He broke the power of sin, ended the reign of death, and took the victory from the grave (1 Corinthians 15:54-57).

When Jesus cried out on the cross, "It is finished." He meant it. And it was finished. The effects and consequences of Adam and Eve's fall in sin were finished. Redemption. Salvation. Freedom. Healing. Deliverance. It was finished.

With victory secured through the resurrection and ascension, Jesus left the ecclesia in the spirit of these words which He spoke in a parable; *"Occupy until I come."* (Luke 19:13 KJV).

The cosmic struggle between the natural and the spiritual, between light and darkness, poverty and prosperity came to an end. The prophetic word that God spoke to the serpent in the garden was completely fulfilled:

"I will put enmity between you and the woman, and between your seed and her Seed; He shall bruise your head, and you shall bruise His heel." (Genesis 3:15 NKJV).

Jesus flawlessly executed every order given to Him by His Father.

"It is finished."

Then Jesus stood as the victor, the conqueror, the king on an unnamed mountain and gave these commands to His occupying armies,

"...All authority has been given to Me in heaven and on earth. Go therefore and make disciples of all the nations, baptizing them in the name of the Father, and of the Son and of the Holy Spirit, teaching them to observe all things that I have commanded you, and lo, I am with you always even to the end of the age." (Matthew 28:18-20 NKJV).

Several biblical commentators suggest that the five hundred along with the eleven apostles were on this mountain when Jesus gave them the orders that would define their occupying the earth and enforcing the victory He secured on the cross.

They were given authority to occupy the nations of the earth from the One who had authority. Authority is exercising the right to rule over and administrate over a specific jurisdiction. It is the ability that is given to exercise specific actions. A government gives authority to those who are submitted to the head.

The authority Jesus possessed was given to His ecclesia, His community, His church. They had authority, but they had to wait for power. On the day of Pentecost, Holy Spirit came and filled them, and they received power to be witnesses. Authority is the right to rule and administrate; power is the ability to do it.

The ecclesia became an occupying force of witnesses operating in authority given from the conquering Lord. With this authority, the ecclesia operates in many spheres, two of which are the sphere of ministry and the sphere of the marketplace. A sphere is a space or place where one has influence. A place that has been assigned to you to carry out your assignment. It is a measure where you live out your call, gifts, and abilities. 2 Corinthians 10:16 identifies a sphere as a place where one is set to accomplish something.

I want to share about two spheres that I see many are called to operate in. Although I am speaking about myself, I believe my story could be your story.

When I was seventeen years old, I recognized and acknowledged the call of God on my life to preach. The call was first revealed to me on a Sunday morning in January 1984. I awakened that morning, and as I laid there, I heard the audible voice of the Lord, the only time I've heard Him in that way. He said, "Stand and preach My word of righteousness." It was a still small voice, but thirty-six years later, I can still hear it.

A few weeks later, the Lord visited me in a dream and showed me the many seasons of darkness I would walk through as a preacher. Seasons of demonic presence, spiritual blindness in the people I would minister to, sin and wickedness in the church, worldliness, and carnality. But I also saw many little fires amid the darkness. They were prophetic symbols (though I didn't know it at the time) of the presence of God manifested in His people and in many places I would travel to. They were the word of God setting His people aflame, and they were symbols of His glory. It would be many years before I knew the meaning of this dream, but that morning, I submitted to the call.

I have learned some things about occupying this sphere that I received from the Lord when I was seventeen. In this space, I am a doorkeeper, and my ministry is a door that opens for men to enter and experience the Savior. My preaching serves as a key that opens the door.

In ministry, I am a warrior and a watchman. I fight by occupying my sphere, standing in it (Ephesians 6:13). This war is the good fight of faith (1 Timothy 6:12). I am not overcoming, I am already an overcomer. I have overcome the devil, the world, and the flesh. Jesus overcame on the cross. I overcome by standing in my sphere.

As a watchman, I watch for the now move of God, and I watch for the future. I watch for the glory to manifest in my sphere. I guard the treasures that have been given to me as a scribe instructed in the kingdom of heaven (Matthew 13:52). I am a creative watchman. I see through my prophetic eyes and my holy imagination what the Lord is doing in the earth and what He has called me to create with Him.

Twenty-eight years after I said yes to the ministry of preaching, the Lord revealed to me that I was an apostle, and my assignment was to build sons for Him, an eternal house that would never end (Ephesians 2:21-22). Each year since He has revealed to me how He desires me to build His house. These sons (not natural but spiritual; male and female) were given to me to impart His word, His truth in them. I was called to help them find their identity as I found mine in the summer of 2012 in the School of the Scribe led by Apostle Theresa Harvard Johnson. I was called to help them mature, not by filling their heads with information but filling their hearts with revelation.

In 2016, I left the denomination I'd been a part of for forty years. Though my assignment was clear, and my ministry sphere distinguishable, I still faced many adversities. Many of the people I was called to were religious and deceived. They were full of tradition and puffed up in pride. Their eyes were dim, and their hearts were dull. The Lord kept sending them, and I kept imparting in them. Most of them left, but a few stayed. Nonetheless, I've found freedom in the sphere of ministry.

I also operate in the sphere of the marketplace. As a creative coach, I try to help creatives see the difference between ministry and the marketplace. Though the same principles can apply, the outcome is quite different. Ministry is about bringing people to an encounter with the Lord. The market is a place of exchange between seller and buyer. Goods and services are exchanged. Agreements are made that involve work and wages. Creativity is profitable because there is an audience that wants the finished product.

When I was forty-two years old, I achieved a dream I had when I was a boy. At ten years old, I wanted to be a published writer, an author. I wanted to be like my hero Alex Haley. In 1977, my mother bought me his book Roots. After reading that book and learning about Alex Haley, a seed was planted in my heart to write the kind of stories I loved to read and to share my gift with people all over the world.

Thirty-two years later, the dream became a reality. I wrote and published my first book. I was called to preach as a boy, and I was called to publish as a man. The Lord told me I would learn how to operate in dominion through publishing. For years, I called it my ministry, but I was wrong. It was not ministry, it was business, and therefore, it was marketplace. Again, there is a difference. We must know what it is if we are to occupy both spheres successfully.

In the absence of this fundamental understanding, I have seen many turn ministry into business and then corrupt it because they bring the wrong understanding to it. Again, ministry is an encounter that causes one to experience the Lord while business (marketplace) is the exchange of ideas, goods and services.

Let me end by giving you one more example. When Joseph was the steward of Potiphar's house, he was in business. When he was Prime Minister over Pharaoh's kingdom, Joseph was in business. When he interpreted Pharaoh's dream, that was ministry.

Why did I call Joseph's interpretation of Pharaoh's dream ministry? Because Joseph operated according to a spiritual gift, and with it, he caused Pharaoh to know God. Joseph had no expectation of being paid for his interpretation. He simply flowed in the gift of God within him, and Pharaoh recognized God in him (Genesis 41:38). As Prime Minister, Joseph increased Pharaoh's wealth because of his business acumen (Genesis 41:55-57; 47:13-26). I am sure that because of his stewardship over Pharaoh's kingdom, Joseph probably became very wealthy himself.

Whatever sphere you are called to, I commend you and encourage you to do well and accomplish much.

◆ ◆ ◆

Bernard Boulton is a creative and instructional writer who is committed to fathering, strengthening, and awakening the creative community to its fullest potential. He has published twelve books, countless articles and delivered empowering messages challenging the creative community to rise out of cycles of complacency, compromise, and oppression to inherit their designated roles as watchmen in the Kingdom.

Bernard, who is an ordained pastor, has preached the Gospel for over thirty-four years nationally and in the nations of Haiti and Nigeria. He holds an Associate's Degree in Biblical Theology and has been Certified to Teach *The Scribal Anointing®* since 2012. Currently residing in Atlanta, GA, Bernard is the overseer of the Watchman on Walls International Fellowship which meets regularly to empower, motivate, mobilize and root creative artists in God's word and eternal purpose. He is also the founder and CEO of Riverlife Publishing Company and the Creative Awakenings Academy, where he equips leaders in succeeding in ministry and the marketplace.

Connect with Bernard at:
www.creativeawakenings.us

About the Compiler

◆

Andrea M. Renfroe is a proven servant-leader with over twenty-five years of marketplace and ministry experience.

As a professional, Andrea was an active duty Marine for over 11 years serving as a Military Police Officer and staff auditor. Thereafter, she served as a government auditor with the Air Force Audit Agency and a Grants and Contracts Fiscal Coordinator for The College of Southern Maryland. She is currently a senior associate for an accounting firm in Virginia.

Andrea is the founder of Kingdom Ventures LLC, a single source business and management consulting firm where she acquaints people, businesses, and organizations with their potential. She is also the founder of Life Keys Training Center, an organization she established to help unlock and develop (build) whole people who impact and transform their respective areas of influence. LKTC's signature program, *The Transformation Encounter*™, is a 90-day journey of mind renewal that leads to a balanced, fully functional and well-managed life. Additionally, *Scribes Mobilize*, LKTC's exclusive scribal program is where Andrea facilitates transformation by:

1. Awakening and connecting scribes to their biblical history and legacy,

2. Grounding and stabilizing scribes in their prophetic identity; and

3. Activating and launching scribes into their present-day responsibilities.

Andrea holds a Bachelor's of Science in Accounting from Hawaii Pacific University, a Masters of Business Administration from Webster University, a Grants Management certificate from *Management Concepts®*, and has been certified to teach *The Scribal Anointing®* since 2016. She's also a certified coach, teacher and trainer with the John Maxwell Team.

Andrea is a Syracuse, New York native. She has two adult children and resides in Oxon Hill, MD with her husband, Telly.

Enduring Excellence

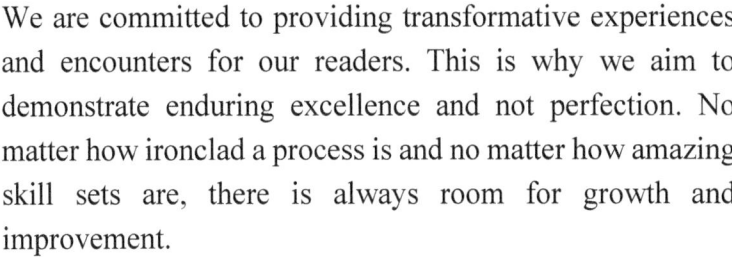

We are committed to providing transformative experiences and encounters for our readers. This is why we aim to demonstrate enduring excellence and not perfection. No matter how ironclad a process is and no matter how amazing skill sets are, there is always room for growth and improvement.

Errors run the gamut as they can be as small as a missing period or question mark and as enormous as perverted teaching. While one error my cause a slight disturbance in the flow of a sentence or paragraph, another error may completely derail a person's life. This is why we approach the publishing process with reverence and our readers with genuine care and concern.

While this publication was subject to the normal publishing rigors and scrutiny in addition to prophetic critiquing, it may still contain some errors. Therefore, we solicit your assistance in helping us maintain our standard of excellence. Please let us know if you find any errors and let us know how we are doing. Please send your findings and comments to: thepropheticpenpublishing@gmail.com.

The Prophetic Pen Publishing Team

For more information about Andrea's initiatives and endeavors, visit:

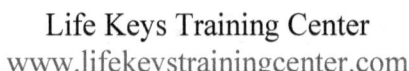

Life Keys Training Center
www.lifekeystrainingcenter.com

Scribes Mobilize
www.lifekeystrainingcenter.org/scribes-mobilize

The Prophetic Pen
www.thepropheticpen.org

Kingdom Ventures, LLC
www.kingdomventuresllc.com

Also written by Andrea

Come Forth: From the Shadows into View
A Poetry Collection

Inspired: A Narrative and Poetry Collection

For more information about *The Scribal Anointing*® and its progenitor, Apostle Theresa Harvard Johnson, visit:

The Voices of Christ Apostolic-Prophetic School of the Scribe
www.thescribalanointing.com

Online School of the Scribe
members.schoolofthescribe.net/courses

The Chamber of the Scribe
www.chamberofthescribe.com

Scribal Prophets
www.facebook.com/groups/scribalprophets

The Scribal Arsenal
www.bookstore.schoolofthescribe.com

www.ingramcontent.com/pod-product-compliance
Lightning Source LLC
Chambersburg PA
CBHW072058290426
44110CB00014B/1728